San Diego:

Ten Ways to Enjoy The Best Food, Beaches and Locations While On Vacation

By

Paul G. Brodie

San Diego: Ten Ways to Enjoy The Best Food, Beaches and Locations While On Vacation

Copyright @ 2017 by Paul G. Brodie

Editing by Devin Rene Mooneyham

All rights reserved in all media. No part of this book may be used or reproduced without written permission, except in the case of brief questions embodied in critical articles and reviews.

The moral right of Paul G. Brodie as the author of this work has been asserted by him in accordance with the Copyright, Designs, and Patents Act of 1988.

Published in the United States by BrodieEDU Publishing, 2017.

Disclaimer

The following viewpoints in this book are those of Paul Brodie. These views are based on his personal experience over the past forty two years on the planet Earth, especially while living in the great state of Texas.

The intention of this book is to share his story about San Diego and what has worked for *him* through this journey.

All attempts have been made to verify the information provided by this publication. Neither the author nor the publisher assumes any responsibility for errors, omissions, or contrary interpretations of the subject matter herein.

This book is for entertainment purposes only. The views expressed are those of the author alone and should not be taken as expert instruction or commands. The reader is responsible for his or her future action. This book makes no guarantees of future success. However by following the steps that are listed in this book the odds of having a great vacation to San Diego definitely have a much higher probability.

Neither the author nor the publisher assumes any responsibility or liability on the behalf of the purchaser or reader of these materials.

The views expressed are based on his personal experiences within the corporate world, education, and everyday life.

This book is dedicated to my mom, Barbara "Mama" Brodie. Without her support and motivation (and incredible cooking) I would literally not be here today

Table of Contents

Free Audiobook Offer

Foreword by Barbara Brodie

Free Webinar Invitation

Introduction

Free Travel Guide

Chapter 1 Where to Stay in San Diego

Chapter 2 Flights and Car Rental

Chapter 3 Grocery Shopping

Chapter 4 Sunsets

Chapter 5 Beaches

Chapter 6 Restaurants and Desserts

Chapter 7 Best Places to Buy Souvenirs

Chapter 8 Excursions -- San Diego Padres, San Diego Zoo, and USS Midway

Chapter 9 Locations to Visit

Chapter 10 Cameras and Other Items to Bring

Conclusion

More Books by Paul

About the Author

Acknowledgments

Contact Information

Feedback

Free Audiobook Offer

Are you a fan of audiobooks? I would like to offer you the audiobook of Motivation 101 for free. All you need to do is go to my website at www.BrodieEDU.com/freeaudiobook and provide your e mail address in exchange for the free digital download. The audiobook will only be available on the website for a limited time as I offer free goodies to my readership on a regular basis.

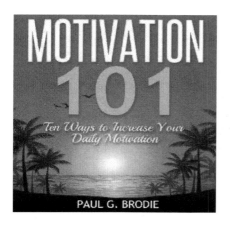

Foreword by Barbara Brodie

I am very proud that Paul has written another book on travel. He spends many hours researching every vacation that we take for the best food, beaches, and locations to ensure the best trip possible. Paul also reaches out to locals and for this book received advice from multiple current and former San Diego residents. I was so impressed with his research, that I suggested that his next book be a travel guide about San Diego. Previously, he wrote a book about Maui I encouraged him to write.

The information has proven to help many people enjoy their vacation to Maui even more and I know this book will help you enjoy San Diego.

I hope that you enjoy reading his book as we had a wonderful time doing many of the things he covers in the book, from visiting the USS Midway and San Diego Zoo, to discovering our own favorite beach in La Jolla, all which he will share in this book. The food throughout the trip was excellent and Paul covers every meal we had with lots of pictures in the book. It will definitely make you hungry and ready to enjoy many of the things that San Diego has to offer.

Enjoy,

Barbara "Mama" Brodie

Arlington, TX

Free Webinar Invitation

Are you looking to publish and market your book to bestseller status in the next 90 days?

I want to invite you to watch my Get Published Webinar.

If you are looking to write your own book on travel, business, self-help, or anything else related to non-fiction then this webinar will help you.

The webinar will also help those who are writing fiction and children's books.

Entrepreneurs, the benefits of writing and publishing a book is an ideal way to build your business and having a book will help you become an authority in your specific area of expertise.

This is what you will learn on this Free Online Workshop:

How to turn your book into multiple revenue streams

How to get your manuscript turned into an eye-catching book

How to market your book including several promo companies that I continue to use two years after publishing my first book

WARNING: The Webinar is only available for a limited time.

Go to www.BrodieEDU.com and click on the Free Webinar tab to sign up today

Introduction

Welcome to San Diego! I wrote this book during the summer of 2017 about my stay in San Diego. It was my first vacation to San Diego and an incredible trip. The trip was organized as our annual family vacation. Each year I take my mom on a family vacation and we chose San Diego due to the beaches, great food, and amazing sightseeing opportunities. My intention with this book is to help with your future vacation to San Diego! We will cover ways to enjoy the best food, beaches, and locations.

One of the biggest challenges about going on vacation is planning the trip. There are ranges of challenges from where to stay and in what type of accommodation you prefer, booking flights, and car rentals, which restaurants to eat at, and choosing whether to book a tour or explore San Diego on your own. You will also notice there are not a lot of books out there that cover what to do in San Diego to maximize your experience.

I will provide you with the necessary tools to have the best vacation experience as possible, while enjoying one of the most beautiful locations in the United States. This book will not only save you money on your vacation, but will also help enhance your experience. The cost of this book will pay for itself many times over.

One thing I want to make clear is that this is a guidebook written by someone who went to San Diego and spent many hours researching the trip, who wants to share his journey with you to help on your next trip. I mention this because this is NOT a Fodor's guide or any other usual guidebook. This book will cover my journey to San Diego and how it can benefit you.

The ideal timeline for the trip is 7-8 days and I cover many great things to enjoy. I have also included a travel guide that will help you including several links that offer close to 100 different things to do in San Diego. My goal is to make the information provided in the book as current as possible.

Restaurants and different locations change over time and this book will be the most current of any books that are available about San Diego. I am also going to cover our favorite restaurants and dessert places from the trip. This includes restaurants for both a late breakfast/early lunch and dinner. There are pictures of every meal so be warned that this book will make you hungry for all of the great food that San Diego has to offer.

Many hours of research went into planning this epic vacation to San Diego. I also received help from multiple people from San Diego and friends that used to live there. Again, a lot of time was spent making this trip the best possible and I am confident that this book will greatly help you on your next trip to San Diego.

Items in the travel guide include travel trips, maps of San Diego, stunning sunset pictures, a map of San Diego beaches, and a detailed ranking of my favorite restaurants in San Diego.

Chapter 1 will cover where to stay in San Diego and the difference between staying at condos and hotels.

Chapter 2 is dedicated to one of the most important parts of planning your trip - booking flights and car rentals.

Chapter 3 covers grocery shopping. There are suggestions for the best places to shop and where to get the cheapest gas in San Diego that will help you pay for this book many times over.

Chapter 4 is dedicated to sunsets. San Diego sunsets, in my view, are amazing. I will share different places to see amazing sunsets while in San Diego.

Chapter 5 explores great beaches. San Diego offers some of the best beaches in the United States and each is unique.

Chapter 6 is about enjoying great restaurants and desserts. San Diego offers wonderful dining. Included is detailed information about every meal from the trip including pictures and how you can enjoy great meals on any budget for breakfast, lunch, dinner, and dessert.

Chapter 7 is dedicated to finding the best souvenirs in San Diego.

Chapter 8 includes excursions to the USS Midway, San Diego Zoo, and San Diego Padres Baseball.

Chapter 9 details visiting three of my favorite locations in San Diego with La Jolla, Coronado Island, and Balboa Park.

Chapter 10 goes over what to bring in regards to cameras and other items to help maximize your vacation.

I hope that this book helps you in your journey to visit San Diego. My philosophy in anything I do in life, whether it's teaching, giving motivational seminars, book publishing, and coaching my book publishing clients is to have the power of one. The power of one is my goal to help at least one person. I hope that person is you.

Free Travel Guide

Would you like a free travel guide that includes maps of San Diego, travel tips, maps of San Diego beaches, and a detailed ranking of Paul's favorite San Diego Restaurants?

Go to www.BrodieEDU.com/SD to download your free travel guide

Chapter 1 Where to Stay in San Diego

I prefer to stay near the beach so we chose a condo that was eight blocks from Pacific Beach. There were a lot of restaurants and shops nearby. The area is busy as San Diego has gotten quite crowded over the past few years.

There are many areas in San Diego to choose from including Pacific Beach, Ocean Beach, Mission Beach, La Jolla, Coronado, and other parts of San Diego. They will vary in price and the closer to the beach, the more expensive it will get.

The locations previously mentioned are those that people tend to frequent the most. The condo we stayed at was very nice and had plenty of room, one bedroom, sleeper sofa in the living room, a kitchen with all the amenities, and a nice sized living room.

I chose to book the trip by booking everything separately. My goal was to really have a custom and unique experience. The condo was found on Airbnb for $200.00 a night with free parking, which to me was a great value with close proximity to the beach and restaurants. I highly recommend researching both Expedia and Airbnb for the best value for how you want to book your trip. Expedia will have combo deals with air and boarding, but I found the best deal for this trip by booking everything separately.

If you would like to use Airbnb and get forty dollars off your stay, then go to www.airbnb.com/c/paulb7435 to sign up. The offer is valid for first time users of Airbnb.

When it comes to choosing your location, you need to look at the following factors: How close you want to stay in proximity to the beach? Cost, how much are you willing to spend?

There are a lot of sites to choose from to book your trip from Airbnb, Expedia, Kayak, Trip Advisor, Priceline and many others.

Chapter 2 Flights and Car Rental

Now that you have decided on a location and hopefully found a great deal for accommodations, it's time to look at booking separate or combo deals for flights and car rental.

After looking at flights for several days, I knew that I wanted to fly Southwest since they were offering a great deal. I was able to get both flights non-stop from Dallas to San Diego for $250.00 each, which was a great deal. The only catch in those prices is that typically they are early or late flights. I prefer that option as it gives me more time on vacation as I typically will book an early flight on the trip outbound and then a late flight on the return home.

I wanted to maximize our trip and my goal was to have as much time in San Diego as possible. Our flight out of Dallas left at 6:20 am Central time and we arrived in San Diego at 7:15 am Pacific time and 9:15 am Central Time. We essentially got an additional day in San Diego with the travel times. For the flight back to Dallas I booked the flight that departed San Diego at 6:00 pm Pacific time on July 4 and landed back in Dallas at 10:55 pm Central time. By doing this we got nine days for our trip even with the travel.

During my research I also found the best prices to be on the airline websites. I researched multiple airlines and we chose to go with Southwest. Again, you can also use many popular travel sites including Expedia, Kayak, Trip Advisor, Priceline and many others.

One thing I have learned during the trip to San Diego was to use a different tactic when renting the car. Originally, I was planning to use UBER and Lyft ridesharing services, but after further research on all the places I wanted to see, decided to rent a car instead.

When I was in Maui in summer 2016 I took a close look at all of the car rental fees from renting at the airport. During that time I checked pricing at the local Enterprise-Rent-A-Car in Kihei (the town where we stayed) and realized that I could have saved between 100-150 dollars on the rental if I would have gone through a regular location to rent the car instead of the airport.

With that in mind, I went to multiple car rental websites and compared the rates between renting at both the airport and at a local location in Pacific Beach. I found a $150.00 dollar savings by renting in Pacific Beach. When we arrived in San Diego we took an Uber to the Enterprise-Rent-A-Car in

Pacific Beach and got a mid-size car rental for $264.00 for the eight days including fees, which was well worth it as it would have cost $400.00 at the airport with fees.

This is definitely an option worth researching and should save you a significant amount of money. I spent $30.00 on two Uber rides to get to and from the airport so the savings are significant. Here is a discount code you can use with Uber to get a free ride up to ten dollars https://www.uber.com/invite/paulb17778ue and another discount code from Lyft for a free ride up to fifteen dollars https://www.lyft.com/invite/paul352064.

Another thing to do is to call your insurance company to see if your current coverage will cover you in your rental car. The car rental company will offer you their insurance. When I worked for Enterprise after college I sold a lot of the insurance and you will most likely not need the additional coverage. Check with your insurance company to find out for sure.

The car we rented ended up being an upgrade to a Chrysler 200 and was a good car for the trip. Parking is a big issue in San Diego and parking spots are pretty small. I drive an SUV, but after researching opted to drive a smaller car and it was a wise decision.

I also recommend a great site called Auto Slash which can be accessed at www.AutoSlash.com. The site will continually look for cheaper car rates and automatically rebook your rental if booked with them and they find a lower rate.

One other thing I would advise, is if you are not pleased with your car then tell the rental car company when you return the car at the end of your trip. Last year in Maui, I turned in the Murano I rented and asked to speak with a manager about the whole experience and how I received the Murano in the rough condition it was given to me. I was originally given a Lincoln Navigator and part of the sunroof fell off and hit me in the head. I brought the SUV back and they switched me out to a Nissan Murano, which is the SUV that I drive at home. The Murano had a lot of dents on it and was a little dirty. By that point I was tired from a ten-hour flight and decided to take the SUV since I was familiar with the SUV. They ended up taking $200.00 off the cost of the rental. Therefore, talking to someone when returning your car can be well worth it, especially if you had any issues with the vehicle.

Chapter 3 Grocery Shopping

Once you have landed and have your car rental, the next best thing to do is to go grocery shopping. San Diego has many grocery stores ranging from Trader Joe's, Vons, Rite Aid, CVS, Costco and Walmart. If you do not have a Costco membership, I highly recommend getting one either before leaving or upon arrival. One of the main reasons is gas and an outstanding return policy. I paid $2.49 a gallon at Costco compared to $2.79 to $3.59 anywhere else. The membership does cost $55.00 for a year but it more than pays for itself, especially in San Diego where prices can get a little pricy depending where you are shopping.

I will warn you that Costco is very, very busy. That is due to both the locals and visitors shopping there. We went multiple times throughout the trip and it was always busy no matter how early we arrived. Parking is also challenging as it took me 10-15 minutes to find a parking spot each time.

One of the other great benefits of Costco is the return policy. It is very generous and their staff even encourage you to return certain items if you need to. We went to Costco both to get gas and to find two beach chairs and two beach umbrellas. I spoke to one of the supervisors and asked about their return policy in case I was unable to take the items back home with me. He actually told me to return the items if the shipping costs ended up costing too much.

Sadly, the costs were too much to ship back and we did return the chairs and umbrellas before the trip ended. The nice thing about Costco is their return policy because the quality of the items and the discount pricing is better than any other beach chairs and umbrellas that you will find in a CVS or other location.

For food we bought most of it at Trader Joe's. There was a location two blocks from the condo and only a short drive. During the trip we ate out for almost every meal. This was due to wanting to try as many restaurants as possible so we didn't buy much food for the condo. I brought Cappuchino pods from home and bought fruit and a few desserts from Trader Joe's.

One other thing I suggest is getting cash back at the stores instead of having to use an ATM and getting hit with ridiculous fees.

Chapter 4 Sunsets

Sunsets in San Diego can be incredible and the best part is they are free. There are many places to see sunsets across San Diego. Regardless of location the sunsets look good wherever you are in San Diego.

The beaches are where we caught most of the sunsets and depending on the cloud cover, are impressive. My favorite beach to watch sunsets is La Jolla Shores. It is also my favorite beach to go to in the San Diego area.

This picture was from the second day of the trip and was from La Jolla Shores Beach.

It was a cloudy day and we were lucky that it cleared up a little.

Here is a picture from Pacific Beach on one of the cloudy days. It was earlier in the sunset and was very cloudy.

Here is a picture of one of the best sunsets I have seen and it was from La Jolla Shores Beach.

As you can see, the sunsets can be impressive depending on the cloud cover. On this evening, we were very lucky as there were very few clouds out. Any of the beaches will provide enjoyable sunsets with varying degrees of cloud coverage and it is worth checking out on your vacation to San Diego.

Chapter 5 Beaches

San Diego has great beaches all over. The main beaches are Pacific Beach, Mission Beach, Ocean Beach, Coronado Beach, La Jolla Shores.

This picture is from Mission Beach and was taken in the early afternoon.

My two favorite beaches during the trip were La Jolla Cove Beach and Mission Beach. La Jolla Shores is one mile long and includes Kellogg Park. The waves are smooth and a lot of families are at the beach. It is a safe area and the sunsets are great. There is also a lot of parking spaces, which is rare for the San Diego area. No matter how busy the beach was, we had no problem finding a good parking spot.

Mission Beach features two miles of coastline and is great if you are looking for lots of different fun things to do. I highly suggest parking at Belmont Park when going to Mission Beach. The beach is very busy and parking can be a challenge. Mission Beach also features a large boardwalk that you can walk, skate, or ride a bike on. Belmont Park has a lot of parking and you should be able to get a parking spot within 5-15 minutes of arriving. After enjoying the beach for a few hours, we put the chairs and umbrellas back in the car and walked over to Belmont Park. The amusement park and entertainment complex has free admission and you buy tickets to access the rides. You can also buy a wristband for unlimited rides for the day. You can order the unlimited ride wristbands in advance on their website www.belmontpark.com at a discounted rate or in person when you get to Belmont Park. They have a huge roller coaster called Giant Dipper Roller Coaster, midway style games that you would see at any state fair or boardwalk, laser tag, a zip line, mini golf. They also have bumper cars, rock climbing, and a small train car that goes around the amusement area for kids and their parents.

Here is a picture of me after playing the feats of strength midway game. It cost $5.00 for three attempts. I was proud of getting the prize and my shoulders were only sore for a couple of hours afterwards.

They also have restaurants and fast food places at Belmont Park. My favorite place was the Sweet Shoppe. It was an ice cream parlor and had the largest portions I have seen. Here is the picture of the double dip ice cream waffle bowl that we split.

The bowl cost eight dollars, but you do get your money's worth. It also helps you cool down as the sun is very strong in San Diego, even at only 70-75 degrees.

Pacific Beach is the largest beach in San Diego and the busiest. It is also very difficult to find parking and was why La Jolla Shores and Mission Beach are both better options in my view. One of my favorite parts about Pacific Beach is the World Famous restaurant. I will cover the food locations more in the next chapter, but World Famous located on Pacific Beach and offers amazing views of the beach and during sunset.

This was the view from our table at World Famous.

Ocean Beach has shopping, restaurants and a dog beach. There were many people with their dogs at the beach when we visited at sunset so if you are a dog person, it is a great beach to check out. They also have volleyball, fishing locations, and surf breaks.

Coronado beach is on Coronado Island. I highly recommend going during the week as the weekends are very busy there with limited parking. We went to Coronado Island on the Saturday of our trip and it was packed. The beach is very nice with a gorgeous shoreline and the Hotel Del Coronado is well worth checking out if you can get a parking spot.

Each of the beaches will have multiple restaurants, and rental locations where you can rent bikes, wet suits, and boogie boards. All of them are nice to go to as all the beaches are spacious even when a lot of people are there. Parking can be challenging so definitely keep that in mind as the wait to find a parking spot can be lengthy depending on where you go.

A few things I would highly recommend bringing for the beach are goggles (and anti-fog liquid solution), two bottles of bottled water, sunscreen, a hat to wear, a swimming shirt if you have pale skin and burn easily (like myself), beach chairs, towels, water, a hard-waterproof small case for your smartphone, keys, driver's license, and cash, a few paper towels, a case for your glasses/sunglasses, and an extra bag for your wet clothes.

My goal was to snorkel during the trip, but unfortunately the water can be quite cold. If you plan on snorkeling I recommend looking into renting or buying a wet suit. The temperatures in the summer are usually between 70-75 degrees and the sun is very warm. However, the ocean temperature is still pretty cold and the trade winds can make it quite cool when you are in the ocean.

The main thing is to enjoy your beach time and be careful as you can burn very easily in the San Diego sun. The beaches across San Diego are beautiful and have multiple opportunities to snorkel, surf, and enjoy fun in the sun.

Chapter 6 Restaurants and Desserts

This is going to be a long chapter so get ready for a lot of great information on some of the best places to eat in San Diego.

San Diego has some of the best restaurants that you will eat at in California or anywhere else. After heading to the beach, we typically went to eat a late breakfast or brunch. There are many great places for breakfast or early lunch that I want to share with you. The first place we went to in San Diego is called the Broken Yolk Cafe. It was a great way to start the trip as it was highly recommended. To get more information about Broken Yolk Café go to www.thebrokenyolkcafe.com. I had the carne asada benedict and my mom got the banana nut pancakes. Below are pictures of both.

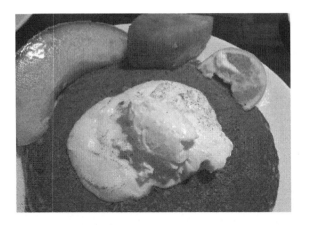

Another great restaurant for a late breakfast or early lunch in Kono's They have two locations in Pacific Beach. The first location is Kono's Surf Club and is next to Pacific Beach. It is a very busy restaurant and parking can be tough to find. Due to that we decided to eat at Konito's Café which is also owned by Kono's. The menu is identical and is located in a shopping center that also has Trader Joes, CVS, and other locations.

The food was excellent and we ordered the big breakfast #1 and big breakfast #2. To get more information about Kono's go to http://www.konoscafe.com. Here are the pictures of two very large breakfast plates, which were both excellent.

The Mission in the Mission beach area was another great place to enjoy breakfast or lunch and was highly recommended by friends in San Diego. It is a busy restaurant and the wait can range from 15-30 minutes, but the wait is well worth it. To get more information about The Mission go to www.themissionsd.com. I had the hash and eggs and my mom had the banana blackberry pancakes with a side order of eggs and bacon. Here are pictures of an amazing breakfast at The Mission.

After thinking that there was no way we could have a better breakfast, along came World Famous. This was another location not only recommended by friends who lived in San Diego, but also multiple Uber drivers and locals I spoke with while on vacation. I am glad I took their advice.

The food was wonderful and the views of Ocean Beach were amazing. World Famous is literally on Pacific Beach and our table was right next to the boardwalk. We had a great breakfast as many people passed by either walking, riding their bikes, or jogging. To get more information about World Famous go to http://www.worldfamouspb.com.

I had the Maine lobster benedict and my mom had their signature Fish N Chips. Here are pictures of breakfast/lunch from World Famous.

The next restaurant is great for lunch or dinner. It is called Slaters 50/50. It is called 50/50 due to offering burger patties that is 50 percent ground beef and 50 percent bacon. If you like burgers I highly recommend Slaters 50/50. I ordered a custom burger, which had a cool order process.

The menus are on your table upon arrival and you also have an order form if you want to make a custom burger. It was fun to make your own burger and I got mine as a 2/3 pound burger with a fried egg, bacon, pickles, and lots of other goodies. Here is a picture of both the order form and burger. My mom also chose a great sandwich with the buffalo chicken sandwich.

This was by far the most indulgent meal of the trip and it was good. I have lost close to 40 pounds this year as far, but I believe that your diet also gets a break while on vacation. With that stated, they also have incredible milkshakes and yes you can customize them. I ordered a shake with Oreo cookies, caramel, and Andes mint chocolate. It tasted like a minty s'more and was delicious. Here is a picture of the shake.

Slaters 50/50 has generous portions and kept us full for the rest of the afternoon. To get more information about Slaters 50/50 go to www.slaters5050.com.

One of the most scenic locations for an early lunch is The Fish Market. The restaurant is next to the USS Midway on the waterfront and offers scenic views of the waterfront. To get more information go to www.thefishmarket.com.

We met up with a good friend of mine for lunch (shout out to Trey Hernandez) who was in the area and had a good lunch. My mom and I both ordered clam chowder to start which was excellent and then Fish N Chips, which also was good. Here are the lunch pictures.

During the trip, we decided to also enjoy Sunday Brunch. After researching multiple restaurants that had a Sunday brunch we chose Tom Ham's Lighthouse. It was one of the best brunches we have ever had and the seafood was incredible. Here is a picture of the seafood plate that I made.

There were many food stations including omelets, seafood, salad, entrees including spare ribs and chicken, a carver station that featured brisket, and of course the dessert station that included a make your own ice cream sundae area.

Here is a picture of some of the breakfast items.

And the ice cream with candy.

The meal costs $48.00 per person and included drinks and unlimited mimosa's. It was a great meal and the best meal of the entire trip.

Tom Ham's Lighthouse is a renovated lighthouse and is beautiful. The views of the lighthouse of San Diego are breathtaking and a great opportunity to take great pictures after brunch. To get more information go to http://www.tomhamslighthouse.com.

I would suggest attempting to book a reservation on their website or by calling the phone number on the website listed above. What I did was attempt to book online a few weeks prior to the trip and was informed they were fully booked. After calling and speaking to the hostess she did say they were fully booked and are booked most of the summer due to the popularity of the restaurant.

The hostess mentioned that you can arrive without a reservation and will be seated within thirty minutes to an hour. I asked the best time to arrive and she suggested 9:30 am when they open. What we did was arrive around 9:20 am. There was already a line outside waiting to get in. The lighthouse has a lot of parking spots so you should be able to get a parking spot.

They opened at 9:30 am and we were able to get seated immediately. The restaurant holds several hundred people and has two floors. If you arrive around 9:20 am like we did, you should be able to get seated almost immediately.

Here is a picture that was taken at Tom Ham's Lighthouse that includes the San Diego skyline.

One of my favorite breakfast items is waffles and I had the best waffle ever during the San Diego vacation. I found this location when researching the trip and it more than lived up to the hype. If you like waffles, then you will love The Waffle Spot. The restaurant is located inside the Kings Inn and isn't the typical location for a great restaurant. You will most likely encounter a wait as the restaurant was busy when we went. We waited thirty minutes and it was well worth it. To get more information go to www.wafflespotsandiego.com.

Originally, I was going to get the double chip waffle, which was a waffle with both white and dark chocolate chips. After talking with one of the customers he highly recommended the churro waffle and referred to it as the best waffle he has ever had. I am glad that I changed my mind as it was one amazing waffle. We both paid an extra $3.50 each to upgrade to the breakfast platter that included eggs, bacon, and sausage. Here is a picture of the churro waffle.

It still makes me crave waffles every time I see that picture. My mom got the banana nut waffle and was also a great choice. Here is a picture of the banana nut waffle.

On our final breakfast/lunch of the trip we were at Balboa Park. After researching the best restaurants in the area, we ended up going to The Prado. They open at 11:30 am and is a great spot for lunch. The dinner menu can get a little pricy, but the lunch menu prices are fair. I had the marinated prime steak panini and my mom had the serrano ham grilled cheese sandwich and tomato basil soup. Both were excellent. Here are the lunch pictures.

The Prado also gives complementary homemade hummus and bread and both were excellent as part of the meal. It was a great lunch and well worth going to if you visit Balboa Park.

The dinners were also excellent. For our first dinner in San Diego we went to Old Town and to the Old Town Mexican Café. I highly recommend getting the street tacos. Here is a picture of the plate.

Due to time, we decided to eat most of our meals out and Old Town was the only place we went to twice. My mom got the chicken chimichanga both times and if you like chicken then you will love the portions.

We went back a second time a week later and mom got the chicken chimichanga and I got the carne asada plate.

The food was excellent on both visits. They are very busy and the servers do not have much time for small talk, but are very efficient. The restaurant will also have people come by and take a picture for you. They give you a free postcard of your picture and then will try to sell you on getting a souvenir version, which you can politely decline or purchase if you want to buy an additional souvenir. To get more information go to www.oldtownmexcafe.com.

The other restaurant which we had twice was The Taco Stand. It is considered one of the best places to get tacos anywhere and I agree. We went to the location in La Jolla and it was amazing. Bought quite a few tacos including carne asada, shrimp, and fish. Here are the pictures.

The tacos were among the best I have ever tasted. Later that week on Saturday I was feeling tired and decided to use door dash, which is a delivery service. I was able to get $5.00 off my order and you can also get $5.00 off your order by checking out door dash at http://drd.sh/sL3xCv. They are basically a delivery version of Uber and I loved using the service. I had the food delivered within an hour and you can also track the order in real time.

For the door dash delivery, a friend recommended that I tried the carne asada fries as that was a unique entrée to try. It was very unhealthy and delicious. Here is a picture of a very unhealthy yet delicious entrée.

Also had the carne asada burrito and mom ordered the shrimp burrito.

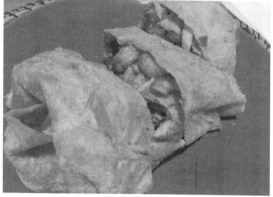

It was nice to have a meal at the condo and door dash was a great way to have food delivered.

San Diego has some of the best Mexican food and throughout the trip we went to as many great restaurants as possible.

One of the highlights of the trip was going to the San Diego Padres baseball game. I will go into more detail in the next chapter, but did want to share what we ate at the ballpark.

Hodad's was one of the places that was highly recommended as they have been a San Diego institution for many years. They have several locations throughout San Diego and they have a location at the ballpark. The menu is more limited at the ballpark due to the amount of people they must serve and the burger was good. I had the bacon cheeseburger basket and my mom had the chicken strip basket. To get more information go to www.hodadies.com. Here are the pictures of the burger and chicken finger basket.

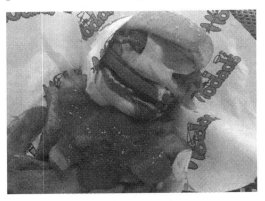

Lucha Libre Taco Shop was another highlight of the trip. The restaurant is named after the Lucha Libre style of professional wrestling in Mexico. They have pictures, Lucha Libre masks, wrestling title belts, and even a table wrestling themed ring in the restaurant. It is a fun place to check out even if you are not a fan of wrestling as they have great food. To get more information go to www.tacosmackdown.com.

I had the carne asada burrito and my mom got the shrimp burrito. Both were huge and tasted great. Here are the food pictures from Lucha Libre.

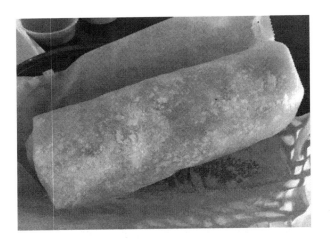

Another great place to get taco's is Oscar's Mexican Seafood. They have several locations across San Diego. We went to the Pacific Beach location and were less than fifty feet from the actual beach. Parking can be challenging in that location and I got lucky with getting one of the few parking spots in front of the restaurant. We bought several tacos including two skirt steak tacos, surf and turf, battered fish, and shrimp. To get more information go to www.oscarsmexicanseafood.com. Here is a picture of the tacos.

We visited La Jolla for a second time later that week and originally were going to go to a restaurant called the Cheese Shop. Unfortunately, they close early on Sunday's so we had to adjust our dinner plans. In La Jolla, a lot of the shops and restaurants close early on Sunday's so finding a restaurant can be challenging. After talking with several residents while walking around La Jolla, the Living Room Coffeehouse was highly recommended. To get more information go to www.livingroomcafe.com.

The food was excellent and the prices were good. The coffeehouse is a European style café and a hookah lounge, which was unique. After speaking with the staff, it was recommended that I try the kabob wrap. The wrap was excellent and am glad that I took their advice. My mom ordered their waffle, which also was great. Here are the pictures of the wrap and waffle.

Every meal we had in the San Diego area ranged from eight to fifteen dollars per person. The only exceptions were Slaters 50/50 and Tom Ham's Lighthouse. Slaters cost twenty per person and Tom Ham's was forty-eight dollars each. The food prices overall were reasonable and San Diego has some of the best food choices around.

In this chapter I have shared with you great restaurants for breakfast, lunch, and dinner. Now I would like to share with you some dessert options.

During our trip, we had dessert several times with a focus on ice cream and gelato. Hammond's Gourmet Ice Cream has one of the most unique options I have seen. They offer a flight of different ice cream flavors. We ended up checking it out after our first dinner of the trip and was well worth it.

Hammond's offers over three hundred flavors of ice cream and sorbet that is made in Hawaii. You can buy a flight of ice cream that includes your choice of five scoops of ice cream and toppings. The ice cream was among the best ice cream that we ever tasted and well worth the ten dollars to buy the flight. To get more information go to www.hammondsgourmet.com.

The flavors chosen were POG (passionfruit, orange, guava), white chocolate macadamia nut, chocolate chunk chunk, mint and cookies, and cotton candy with caramel, whipped cream, and Oreo cookie toppings. Here is the picture of the ice cream sundae flight.

While in La Jolla we went from La Jolla Shores Beach to dinner before going back to the beach to watch the sunset. After having a great dinner at The Taco Strand we went to Bobboi Natural Gelato. It was the best gelato we ever had and was well worth the visit. To get more information go to www.bobboi.com.

Their gelato is all organic and I ordered the large bowl for eight dollars which included three flavors. We went with salted caramel, mint chip, and chocolate caramel. It was delicious and here is the picture.

Before leaving San Diego on July 4 we stopped at Ghiradelli Ice Cream and Chocolate Shop at the Gaslamp Quarter. It is one of my favorite places to have ice cream with previous visits to their San Francisco, Chicago, and Las Vegas locations. We ordered the cookie bits sundae and customized the flavors. The flavors we got were mint chocolate chip, cookie dough, and expresso chip. To get more information go to www.ghirardelli.com. Here is the picture of the awesome customized cookie bits sundae.

We had great desserts on the trip and bought several desserts at Trader Joe's for the condo including dark chocolate covered frozen mango ice cream, Trader Joe's cookie dough ice cream, and a mud pie. All were great and well worth looking into when you are on vacation in San Diego.

This chapter alone in my view is worth the price of the book many times over. A lot of time and research was put into finding the best food in the San Diego area and I feel these restaurants will give you an amazing experience across San Diego.

Chapter 7 Best Places to Buy Souvenirs

There are souvenir shops throughout San Diego and will be easy to find. The costs do vary and after going to multiple shops we ended up buying all of our souvenirs in La Jolla. The souvenir shop is called La Jolla Cove Gifts. To get more information go to https://www.lajollacovegifts.com.

La Jolla Cove Gifts had the best prices that we saw from visiting the different shops throughout the San Diego area including Pacific Beach, Ocean Beach, Mission Beach, Old Town, Coronado, Downtown San Diego, and La Jolla. The gift shop was honored multiples times as the best value in La Jolla. If you happen to be in La Jolla I would highly recommend buying your souvenirs there.

The San Diego Zoo has lots of great souvenirs from stuffed animals to shot glasses, shirts, and other cool items. You will pay a premium, but visiting the San Diego Zoo is a rare opportunity. Same for the USS Midway Museum gift shop as they have lots of cool souvenirs including toy and model fighter jets, helicopters, drinking glasses, coffee mugs, and lots of other items.

Petco Field, home of the San Diego Padres baseball team has lots of baseball related souvenir shops throughout the ballpark including Padres shirts, jerseys, hats, drinking glasses, shot glasses and other items.

Old Town, which is a very touristy yet nice area has multiple souvenir shops where you can find almost anything you can think of in regards to gifts.

The waterfront by the USS Midway museum has many small shops that sell lots of different items including Lucha Libre wrestling masks. The masks also include superheroes from Spiderman, Batman, Deadpool, and Wolverine. You can also buy street art in addition to the usual souvenirs.

Balboa Park has many different souvenir shops and it is easy to find souvenir shops wherever you go in San Diego, but please note you will be paying a premium in certain areas.

Chapter 8 Excursions - San Diego Padres, San Diego Zoo, and USS Midway

San Diego has a lot of different places to visit while on vacation. During the trip, we wanted to see as many of them as possible while also enjoying lots of beach time.

Our first non-beach excursion was to the San Diego Padres baseball game at Petco Park. It was a night game and you might want to consider bringing a light jacket with you as it can get a little cold. The temperature will be in the mid to high 60s during summer games.

Petco Park is one of the nicest looking ballparks. The stadium was half full in terms of attendance so you could either buy tickets on Stub Hub or buy the tickets at the stadium box office. Attendance will vary depending on which team is in town. We went when the Atlanta Braves were visiting due to it being a Wednesday night game and the lower ticket prices. I was able to get club level seats for twenty dollars each and was well worth it.

The Los Angeles Dodgers were playing the Padres that same weekend in San Diego and the prices for those games was almost double as a lot of

Dodgers fan were attending those games due to the close proximity of Los Angeles to San Diego. Attending the game was a lot of fun and it was fun to check out the ballpark. To get more information go to www.mlb.com/padres.

Parking can be expensive for a ballgame and driving to downtown San Diego during rush hour can take a while. Instead of dealing with the traffic and parking, you have some options. There is a trolley system in San Diego that you can park and ride to if you have your own car. The trolley will take you to the ballpark. We went with a different option.

Instead of taking the trolley, we opted for an Uber ride share. The driver picked us up within five minutes of placing the request on the Uber app and the ride cost $17.00 each way. It was well worth it as my mom is a little older and cannot walk for long. With getting the Uber directly to the ballpark entrance it was very helpful.

After the game, we ordered another Uber that picked us up outside the ballpark. Make sure you check the location on the Uber app as the app is not always accurate with your specific ballpark location.

The San Diego Zoo was the best zoo I have ever seen. It is a huge property and has animals from all over the world. One thing they do not advertise is their senior discount. If you are over the age of sixty-five they do offer a discount, but it is not listed on their pricing. You must ask for it when paying for your ticket at their box office.

As part of the entrance price the San Diego Zoo has a forty-minute tour on their tour buses. Due to my mom's struggles with walking a lot we took the bus tour and it was very efficient. You line up at the tour entrance and within fifteen minutes you are on one of the buses. They are double decker buses with the top deck uncovered so bring a hat and sunscreen if you are going to be on the top deck. We chose the lower deck due to the shade.

During the tour, they take you to most of the locations in the zoo and is a great way to see the zoo without walking around too much. After the tour, we stopped for a quick break at one of the restaurants. The prices at the restaurants are a little steep, but air conditioning and cool air was well worth it.

We planned the rest of our time at the zoo at the restaurant and decided to take the Kangaroo Bus to explore the zoo ourselves. The Kangaroo Bus is a tour bus that takes you to a specific location checkpoint at the zoo. They have four checkpoints with each checkpoint listed as one, two, three, or four. We ended up going from checkpoint one to checkpoint two. My mom relaxed at the one of the benches and I explored the area.

The zoo has lots of inclines and a lot of uphill and downhill walking. If you are with someone who cannot do a lot of walking it is important to know that in advance. They also have an Ariel Tram at the checkpoint two area that will take you to the opposite side of the park. I was able to take a round-trip ride and it was a lot of fun. You can see the zoo from up high in addition to downtown San Diego and specifically Balboa Park. The tram is safe for families as well. Here is a picture from my adventure on the tram.

After that excursion, we decided to get the Kangaroo Bus and went to checkpoints three and four. We stayed on the bus, but could see most of the exhibits from both the initial tour and the Kangaroo Bus. Once the Kangaroo Bus went back to checkpoint one we got off the bus and called it a day at the zoo. We ended up staying around four hours total and the zoo was an amazing place to see. To get more information go to http://zoo.sandiegozoo.org.

My favorite excursion was to the USS Midway Museum. We went after brunch at Tom Ham's Lighthouse since it was on the way back to the condo. Tickers for adults are $20.00 at the entrance and is an incredible value. The museum offers senior discounts for entry for $17.00. You can also buy tickets online for an additional discount. To get more information go to www.midway.org.

The museum has twenty-nine restored aircraft, sixty different exhibits, flight simulators, and aircraft that you can go inside of and sit in. My favorite part was the flight deck on the top of the aircraft carrier. Most of the restored aircraft were on the top deck and I felt like I was in the movie, Top Gun. Here are a few pictures from the top deck of the USS Midway.

Out of the different excursions the USS Midway was the most fun and the best value. It is well worth going to and it will make you feel like a big kid again with all the cool aircraft.

Another very popular excursion is Sea World. We were not able to make it to Sea World on this trip. I have previously gone to both the Orlando and San Antonio Sea World locations and loved each trip. To get more information about Sea World go to www.seaworld.com/san-diego.

Chapter 9 Locations to Visit

In Chapter 8 I covered different excursions as San Diego has lots of great entertainment options. I want to cover specific locations to visit in this chapter. My favorite location in San Diego County is La Jolla.

The area is quieter compared to San Diego and La Jolla has in my view the nicest beach in the area with La Jolla Shores. I would highly recommend going to La Jolla when in San Diego. The drive is only fifteen to twenty minutes from Pacific Beach and is in the north part of San Diego County.

As I have covered in previous chapters, the restaurants in the area are excellent as well as the dessert choices. We ended up spending two afternoons and evenings in La Jolla and loved it. It was also where we bought our souvenirs to bring back.

Another area is Coronado Island. The island is beautiful with great views of both the San Diego skyline and the Hotel Del Coronado. There is a high ramp that you drive on to get to Coronado Island and the view is impressive. Once you have arrived on the island I recommend immediately finding the beach area that faces the San Diego skyline and park your car to enjoy the view and take pictures. Here is a picture from the brief stop.

Coronado Beach is on the opposite side of the island from where the picture was taken and is less than a five-minute drive. The beach is beautiful and the Hotel Del Coronado is also on the beach. I would suggest going during the week as it gets very busy on the weekends. We ended up going on Saturday afternoon and parking was not only difficult, but virtually impossible to get. It is much less congested during the week. To get more information about Coronado go to www.sandiego.org/explore/coastal/coronado.aspx.

Balboa Park is another fun area to go to and was how we spent our final day in San Diego. If you need luggage storage for your final day then I recommend using San Diego Airport Luggage Storage. They will store your luggage for a fee while you enjoy the final day in San Diego. To get more information about their service go to http://sdairportluggage.com/content/storage. Balboa Park includes seventeen museums, performing arts venues, multiple gardens including the Japanese Friendship Garden, the San Diego Zoo, multiple shopping options, and much more. For more information about Balboa Park go to www.balboapark.org.

We went to lunch at The Prado first and then explored the area. One of the cool things about Balboa Park is that you can rent bikes and Electriquette Wicker Carts. With my mom's challenges with extended walking I knew a cart would be needed since the park does not offer any other transportation except to and from the parking lot.

I rented the cart for two hours and it was a lot of fun. We were able to check out the San Diego Museum of Art, Timken, Casa del Prado, House of Hospitality, Casa del Balboa, Zoro Garden, Fleet Science Center, and Natural History Museum and many other places in the cart. You can get a discount flyer at the House of Hospitality and they offer both adult and senior rates. To get more information about the carts go to www.wickercarts.com/wp/historical-info. Here is the picture of the cart outside the museum.

The carts are electric and are easy to operate. They have been a part of Balboa Park since 1915. You can easily spend an entire day at Balboa Park as there is lots to see. Each of the museums has admission fees, but you can also walk around Balboa Park or drive your cart around and enjoy the beautiful architecture.

Chapter 10 Cameras and Other Items to Bring

One of the things I am sure you want to do is to record as many memories as possible while in San Diego. The vacation is not cheap and you will want to bring as many great memories and pictures and video as possible during your stay.

I would highly recommend buying a quality camera. Your smartphone will take good pics, but having a quality camera while on vacation will ensure that you have the best quality pictures. Personally, I am biased towards Fuji and bought their newest FinePix S1 model on eBay a week prior to leaving for Maui last year. I also brought two small Kodak High Definition video cameras that I use for my motivational seminars to record footage and to have a backup in case something went wrong with the other camera.

If something does happen to your camera or video camera, I highly recommend going to Costco for a replacement and Walmart as a backup option. I also would suggest bringing extra cameras if possible because incidents and accidents can happen.

In regards to other items, I included several items to bring in my travel guide and would definitely recommend bringing zip ties to use as locks for your luggage when traveling, a nail clipper to put in your backpack to cut the zip tie and to also trim nails. Consider bringing an extra bag for souvenirs for items you want to buy or just buy one at Walmart like I did on my trip to Maui last summer.

Other items include bringing a fleece and a windbreaker if you plan enjoy a Padres game or watch a sunset at the beach as it can get cooler at night. Swimming trunks can be bought at good prices at either Costco or Walmart upon arrival. You will definitely want to bring sandals in addition to shoes as sand literally gets everywhere and it is easier to wear sandals, especially at the beach.

A few other tips include bringing your own snacks for the flight and some small snacks. On this trip, I brought a twelve pack of Keurig cappuccino pods. They came in handy as I was not able to find them at Trader Joes or Vons. I also would recommend taking hand sanitizer, wet wipes, and portable battery power stations for your phone and tablets. Be sure to sign up for flight status alerts and notifications the night before your flight. I would also recommend that you bring an empty water bottle with you (I love the OXO Good Grips 24 oz Two Top Plastic Water Bottle) to fill up once you pass security. I usually get a restaurant to fill it with water compared to using the water fountain.

Conclusion

Through the past ten chapters we have covered a range of topics from where to stay in San Diego, booking flights and car rentals, enjoying beautiful beaches, where to find amazing food in San Diego, excursions including the San Diego Padres, San Diego Zoo, and USS Midway Museum, locations to see including La Jolla, Coronado, and Balboa Park, and the best places to find souvenirs. My hope is that this book can help with your own personal quest to have the best trip possible to San Diego.

I want to thank you for reading my ninth book. Writing each book is a labor of love. I write about things I am passionate about and I believe having a happy, positive and motivated mindset is one of the most important things in life.

If you enjoyed this book and are wondering if you could also write and publish your own travel book, business, self-help, non-fiction, fiction, or children's book then I invite you to check out my free webinar that will help you in your author journey. You can get more information in the table of contents of this book by looking up my free webinar offer.

Stayed tuned for the release of my next book, Book Publishing for Authors: How to Publish and Market Your Book to Bestselling Status in the Next 90 Days and I invite you to check out my other books with the link on the next page. I would like to offer you the opportunity to read the first chapter of my next book, Book Publishing for Authors.

Go to www.BrodieEDU.com/SD to download the first chapter of Book Publishing for Authors

I would also like to offer you the opportunity to read the first chapter of my next travel book about Maui. This is my second book about Maui and will be released soon. Tap the link below to read the first chapter.

Go to www.BrodieEDU.com/SD to download the first chapter of Maui

More Books by Paul

"Quick and inexpensive reads for self-improvement, a healthier lifestyle, and book publishing"

Eight-time Amazon bestselling author, Paul Brodie believes that books should be inexpensive, straightforward, direct, and not have a bunch of fluff.

Each of his books were created to solve problems including living a healthy lifestyle, increasing motivation, improving positive thinking, traveling to amazing destinations, and how to help authors publish and market their books.

What makes Paul's books different is his ability to explain complex ideas and strategies in a simple, accessible way that you can implement immediately.

Want to know more?

Go to www.BrodieEDU.com/Books

About the Author

Paul Brodie is the President of BrodieEDU, an education consulting firm that specializes in giving motivational, business, publishing, and leadership seminars for universities and corporations. He is also the CEO of Brodie Consulting Group, which specializes in book publishing and coaching clients on how to publish and market their books.

Brodie recently left teaching after serving as an educator in multiple roles since 2008. He served as a Special Education Teacher from 2014-2017 in the Hurst-Euless-Bedford ISD (2014-2016) and Fort Worth ISD (2016-2017) while working specifically with special needs children who had Autism. In 2014-2015 he also served as the head tennis coach and lead the school to a district championship and an undefeated season.

From 2011-2014, Brodie served as a Grant Coordinator for the ASPIRE program in the Birdville Independent School District. As coordinator, he created instructional and enrichment programming for over 800 students and 100 parents in the ASPIRE before and after school programs. He also served on the Board of Directors for the Leadership Development Council, Inc. from 2005-2014 with leading the implementation of educational programming in low cost housing.

From 2008-2011, he was a highly successful teacher in Arlington, TX where he taught English as a Second Language. Brodie turned a once struggling ESL program into one of the top programs in the school district. Many of his students moved on to journalism, AVID, art classes, and many students exited the ESL program entirely.

Teaching methods during his career as an educator included daily writing practice, flash cards, picture cards, academic relays, music, movies, and short educational videos including the alphabet and sight words. Additional strategies included graphic novels paired with movie versions of the novels, games, cultural celebrations, and getting parents involved in their children's education. Brodie's approach has been called unconventional but very effective, revolutionary, and highly engaging. His students have always shown great improvement with both academics and behavior throughout the school year and he was honored to teach such an amazing and diverse group of students during his career as an educator.

Previously, Brodie spent many years in the corporate world and decided to leave a lucrative career in the medical field to follow his passion and transitioned into education. Prior to working in the medical field, he worked for Enterprise Rent-A-Car after receiving his Bachelor's Degree and for Savitz Research during his high school and college years. He is very grateful for every career opportunity as each one was an avenue to learn and grow.

Brodie earned an M.A. in Teaching from Louisiana College and B.B.A. in Management from the University of Texas at Arlington. Brodie is a bestselling author and has written eight books. He wrote his first book, Eat Less and Move More: My Journey in the summer of 2015. Brodie's goal of the book was to help those like himself who had challenges with weight. The goal of his first book was to promote not only weight loss but also health and wellness. He is also the author of Motivation 101, Positivity Attracts, Book Publishing for Beginners, The Pursuit of Happiness, Maui, Just Do It and PMA. All eight books (available in Kindle, Paperback, and Audiobook) are Amazon bestsellers and are based on his motivational seminars, book publishing, love of travel, and struggles with weight.

His seminars have been featured at many universities and at leadership conferences across the United States since 2005. Brodie is active in professional organizations and within the community and currently serves on the Advisory Board for Advent Urban Youth Development and as a volunteer with the Special Olympics. He continues to be involved with The International Business Fraternity of Delta Sigma Pi and has served in many positions since 2002 including National Vice President – Organizational Development, Leadership Foundation Trustee, National Organizational Development Chair, District Director, and in many other volunteer leadership roles. He resides in Arlington, TX.

Acknowledgments

Thank you to God for guidance and protection throughout my life.

Thank YOU the reader for investing your time reading this book.

Thank you to my amazing mom, Barbara Brodie for all of the years of support and a kick in the butt when needed. I also want to thank mom for taking the time to write such an outstanding foreword.

Thank you to my awesome sister, Dr. Heather Ottaway for all of the help and feedback with my books and also with my motivational seminars. It is scary how similar we are.

Thank you to Devin Mooneyham for serving as the editor of my ninth book. The slicing and dicing as always was very much appreciated and I could not have gotten this book published without her assistance.

Thank you to Lindsay Palmer who is working tirelessly to get me booked on college campuses for seminars throughout the United States. I could not have a better team of people to work with on Team Brodie.

Thank you to all who have served on the BrodieEDU Advisory Board.

Thank you to my dad, Bill "The Wild Scotsman" Brodie for his encouragement and support with the business aspects of BrodieEDU and Brodie Consulting Group.

Thank you to Shannon and Robert Winckel (two members of the four horsemen with myself and our good friend, Derrada Rubell-Asbell) for their friendship and support. Shannon and Robert are two of my best teacher friends and are always great sounding boards for ideas.

Thank you to (Don) Omar Sandoval for his friendship and help with several BrodieEDU projects including building our awesome website.

Thank you to all of the amazing friends that I have worked with over the past twenty plus years. Each of them has made a great impact on my life.

Thank you to all of my students that I have had the honor to teach over the years. I am very proud of each of my kids.

Thank you to Delta Sigma Pi Business Fraternity. I learned a great deal about public speaking and leadership through the organization and every experience that I have had helped me become the person that I am today.

Thank you to my three best friends: J. Dean Craig, Jen Mamber, and Aaron Krzycki. We have gone through a lot together and I look forward to many more years of friendship.

Thank you to all of the students past and present at the UT Arlington and UT Austin chapters of DSP. Both schools mean a lot to me and I look forward to seeing them again at some point in the near future.

Thank you to the Lott Family (Stacy, Kerry, Lexi, and Austin) for their friendship over the past seven years.

Thank you to Robin Clites for always taking care of things at the house with ensuring that Mom and I can always get that family vacation every year.

Contact Information

Go to www.BrodieEDU.com/seminars to see why you should consider booking Paul for your campus or organization.

Paul can be reached at Brodie@BrodieConsultingGroup.com

Website www.BrodieEDU.com

@BrodieEDU on Twitter

Paul G. Brodie author page on Facebook

Paul G. Brodie author page on Amazon

BrodieEDU Facebook Page

BrodieEDU YouTube Channel

Feedback

Please leave a review for my book as I would greatly appreciate your feedback.

I also welcome you to contact me with any suggestions at
Brodie@BrodieConsultingGroup.com

Made in the USA
Lexington, KY
10 March 2018